Changed in the Waiting

AN ADVENT DEVOTIONAL

Cover Design: Caines Design
Interior Design: Caines Design/Sharon Page

All Scripture quotations, unless indicated, are taken from THE HOLY BIBLE, NEW IN-TERNATIONAL VERSION®, NIV®. Copyright © 1973, 1978, 1984, 2011 by Biblica, Inc.® Used by permission. All rights reserved worldwide.

Scripture quotations marked (MSG) are from *The Message*. Copyright © 1993, 2002, 2018 by Eugene H. Peterson. Used by permission of NavPress. All rights reserved. Represented by Tyndale House Publishers, Inc.

Scripture quotations marked (NRSVUE) are from the New Revised Standard Version, Updated Edition. Copyright © 2021 National Council of Churches of Christ in the United States of America. Used by permission. All rights reserved worldwide.

Scripture quotations marked (NLT) are from the *Holy Bible*, New Living Translation, copyright © 1996, 2004, 2015. Used by permission of Tyndale House Publishers, Inc., Wheaton, Illinois 60189. All rights reserved.

The internet addresses, email addresses, and phone numbers in this book are accurate at the time of publication. They are provided as a resource. The Foundry Publishing does not endorse them or vouch for their content or permanence.

Publication information for the poem quoted in the introduction: Marilyn Chandler McEntyre, "What to Do in the Darkness." Quoted in Holly W. Whitcomb, *Seven Spiritual Gifts of Waiting: Patience, Loss of Control, Living in the Present, Compassion, Gratitude, Humility, Trust in God* (Minneapolis: Augsburg Books, 2005), 38.

10 9 8 7 6 5 4 3 2 1

Contents

On Advent and Waiting

I hate waiting. And this is unfortunate because we humans spend a lot of time doing it.

We wait for our kids to get their shoes on and for the water to boil. We wait for our order to be delivered, impatiently tracking its progress each day or hour or minute of its journey. We wait for red lights to turn green, for fruit to get ripe, for spring to arrive, for labor to begin. So much of our human experience is spent waiting for things we know will eventually happen.

But there's another kind of waiting that's even worse. It's the kind of waiting that doesn't have a finish line or known outcome. This is the kind of waiting that is familiar to parents with estranged children, single adults who long to be married, or those who have suffered the injustice of wrongful conviction. This kind of waiting is heavy, sometimes suffocating. And, although the circumstances vary, it seems this kind of waiting is also built into the reality of human existence. We wait to feel at home in a new community after a big move, or at a new job after being laid off. We wait for a diagnosis, or to see if treatment will work. We wait for the fog of grief to clear, for what is wrong to be made right.

The first kind of waiting reveals our impatience and desire for control. But the second kind of waiting is accompanied by suffering and reveals the deepest longings of our souls. We long for healing, wholeness, justice, and belonging.

Time spent waiting can feel empty and purposeless, as if nothing can move forward until the waiting is over. But Advent honors our waiting with a name and a place in the progression of time. This is the season of waiting. Sometimes we may only think of Advent in terms of the first kind of waiting—we wait for December 25 to arrive, when we can finally sing "Joy to the World!" and open our gifts—but Advent is actually much more about the second kind of waiting. In Advent we not only prepare to celebrate the way Jesus came to earth two thousand years ago, but we also wait for Christ to come *again*. Our deepest desires are given voice as we watch and wait for King Jesus to make all things right, once and for all.

Advent is the first season of the Christian calendar, beginning the new year for the global church. We begin another cycle of time by orienting ourselves to the reality that we are a people *in waiting*. By definition, this means we are a people of expectation and hope—but also of longing and sadness. Perhaps most importantly, it means that we are not people who can *make happen* the things for which we wait. Although we may concede it reluctantly, waiting makes us admit we are not the ones controlling the story we find ourselves in. Even though we may initially resist this truth, it is actually really good news for us because what we need is so much greater than what we can make happen on our own.

When we submit to this reality, our time spent waiting can shape us— if we let it. If we assume that waiting is empty time to be filled with distractions to keep us occupied, we close ourselves off to its transformative possibilities. Change comes as we allow ourselves to sit in the darkness of our waiting and trust that there is more happening than what we can make happen.

The words of poet Marilyn Chandler McEntyre offer some welcome wisdom here.

What to Do in the Darkness

Go slowly
Consent to it
But don't wallow in it
Know it as a place of germination
And growth
Remember the light
Take an outstretched hand if you find one
Exercise unused senses
Find the path by walking in it
Practice trust
Watch for dawn

When we do these things, we find that waiting is not empty time at all. It is full of God's presence, full of our own deepest desires, and full of opportunity to be changed in the waiting. In this space, the fruit of the Spirit may take root and blossom in us. When we stop trying to fill every moment with our own activity and agenda, we grow in awareness and receptivity of *God's* agenda and *God's* activity.

And what is this good work of God's activity and God's agenda? Amazingly, I find that the virtues of the kingdom I am waiting for take shape *in me*. We take on the characteristics of what we love, and the things we love are those for which we are willing to wait. As we name our deepest longings in our waiting, we are shaped more into the kingdom and the King we are waiting for. The virtues of hope, love, joy, and peace are the hallmarks of God's work in all of history and in our very hearts. Advent is marked by these virtues, and in practicing the waiting of Advent, we become marked by them as well. So, although I still hate waiting, I am coming to trust that the Spirit uses time spent waiting to do something good in me.

Even still, we must acknowledge that everyone enters Advent differently. In the decade or more that I've been keeping time with the Christian calendar, I've learned a beautiful and surprising truth. For some of us, the seasons (Advent, Christmas, Epiphany, Lent, Eastertide, and Ordinary Time) help us engage with a reality that would otherwise be easy to ignore. But for others, a particular season names our current experience—perhaps one that has been going on for a long time already.

For some, the invitation to voice our deepest longings while we wait may feel like a jarring disorientation. If this is you, know that being uncomfortable doesn't mean you're doing it wrong; instead, it probably means you're doing it exactly right. Others are well practiced in voicing their longings because they've already been living in a state of waiting for a while. If this is you, I pray this journey through Advent gives you permission to name where you are and that it is sacred.

Whether you have been here for a while or are just arriving, my prayer is that you receive what you need this Advent.

———

The writings offered in these pages are taken from experiences of waiting throughout Scripture, including Lectionary readings for each Sunday of Advent. Reflect throughout each week on what you read, using the questions at the end of each day as a way to journal individually or prompt discussion with family members, housemates, or small group members.

Traditionally the four weeks of Advent are marked by the themes of hope, love, joy, and peace—the promises we hold onto as we wait. But these are not just things to observe from afar; they are the very gifts the Spirit seeks to grow in us as we wait. With this in mind, I offer an invitation to engage with four week-long practices as a way to receive and nurture these gifts. But it's important to remember that these are indeed *practices*, not *performances*. The goal is to become more aware of God's presence and activity in our lives, not ace an assignment. I invite you into a posture of curiosity and receptivity as you engage with the readings, practices, and questions for each week. It's okay if it's unfamiliar or challenging, or if some days click better than others. We trust that the Spirit knows what the Spirit is about, even if we do not.

May we indeed be changed in our waiting.

—*Michaele LaVigne*

DECEMBER 1, 2024

SCRIPTURE

PSALM 25:1–10

In you, Lord my God,
I put my trust.
I trust in you;
do not let me be put to shame,
nor let my enemies triumph over me.
No one who hopes in you
will ever be put to shame,
but shame will come on those
who are treacherous without cause.

Show me your ways, Lord,
teach me your paths.
Guide me in your truth and teach me,
for you are God my Savior,
and my hope is in you all day long.

—PSALM 25:1–5

Sometimes hope gets mislabeled "naivete," or "wishful thinking." But the truest demonstrations of hope tell us nothing could be further from the truth. Hope is not blind, nor does it view the world with rose-colored glasses. Hope lives in the real world and sees things as they actually are, while still holding out for how things *should* be. Hope does not demand cheer, optimism, or constant positivity.

All throughout Scripture, we find that *lament* is the language of those who wait in hope. Psalms, Lamentations, and the Prophets are full of honest, gut-wrenching prayers like this: "My soul is in deep anguish. How long, Lord, how long? I am worn out from my groaning. All night long I flood my bed with weeping and drench my couch with tears" (Psalm 6:3, 6).

This may not sound hopeful, exactly. But if hope is to endure through disappointment, grief, and suffering, it must be given space to be honest.

With the voices of Scripture as our witness, hope is not diminished by the voicing of lament—it is actually strengthened. There is a paradox here that is difficult to explain. We are invited to explore and experience its truth instead.

During this first week of Advent, we will give ourselves to the practice of lament as we are strengthened in hope. Lament is messy. It is raw and emotional. These may not be the kinds of words you would normally use in your prayers or to describe your life. But if we are to be changed in our waiting, we must choose to be fully present, even when life is messy. When we have the courage to enter these deep waters, we find we are in very good company.

QUESTIONS FOR REFLECTION, DISCUSSION, AND PRAYER

How do you define hope for yourself?

....

....

....

....

....

....

....

....

....

....

....

....

When have you witnessed someone else's lament, and what
has been your response to it?

How comfortable are you with voicing your own pain and disappointment?

I Wait for the Lord

SCRIPTURE

PSALM 130

*I wait for the LORD, my whole being waits,
and in his word I put my hope.
I wait for the LORD
more than watchmen wait for the morning,
more than watchmen wait for the morning.*

*Israel, put your hope in the LORD,
for with the LORD is unfailing love
and with him is full redemption.
He himself will redeem Israel
from all their sins.*

—PSALM 130:5-8

Because you can't really hope for something you already have, hope and waiting go hand in hand. Acknowledging that waiting is hard gives us permission to say that hope is often hard too.

I have a friend whose last five years have been spent walking with her teenage son through a debilitating chronic illness, while also caring for three other children, two of whom have separate disability diagnoses, and most recently her mom, who has brain cancer. She knows something about being up all night with the watchmen, longing for change to come with the sunrise. She is my resident expert in hope.

Her definition of hope is made up of three equal parts: one-third is acknowledging that things are not how you wish they were; one-third is deciding not to resign yourself to how things are now; and one-third is recognizing you're not actually in charge of the outcome. As I have been privileged to witness her journey, I have seen that hope is a struggle. More than an emotion, it is a commitment to live in the tension of waiting while caring deeply about the outcome. It takes effort to stay engaged rather than check out, give up, or distract yourself from your painful reality while you wait for it to change.

While our English word does little to help us grasp these complexities of hope, the Hebrew words *qavah* and *yahal* provide better insight. These words found throughout the psalms are at times translated as "hope" and other times as "wait." In Psalm 130, *qavah* is used twice and is translated above as "wait." *Yahal* is also used twice and is translated as "hope." In yesterday's scripture, though, some versions translate *yahal* as "hope" while others use "wait." This seeming fluidity is because the concept of hoping and waiting are two sides of the same coin in Hebrew thought.

Qavah is a verb meaning "to wait," and it is used to form the noun *tiqvah*, which means "hope." *Qavah* is also connected with concepts of tension, twisting, stretching, endurance, and strength. There is relationship implied here—the word itself bears witness to ancient wisdom. Waiting in uncertainty creates a tension that stretches the one who is willing to hold on, and that can produce an ever-strengthening endurance.

Yahal also carries the meaning of waiting and expectation. In both instances, waiting leads to hope only in reference to the one for whom we wait. Without the knowledge that the one on whom we wait can be trusted, the waiting is not hopeful at all. Waiting on *God* allows us to hope. But trust and hope do not displace the painful tension of waiting.

We are given evidence throughout Scripture that hope can coexist with anger, pain, and disappointment. The prophets and psalmists certainly did not pretend to be happy about the waiting they were doing. Their words of anguish and hope twisted together can give us the courage to voice our own. Jesus himself used the psalms to voice his lament!

Many of us have believed there is no room for sadness if we trust in God, but this is not the message of Scripture. Because waiting is so hard, and because our God can be trusted, we can voice our lament and our hope all in one breath.

QUESTIONS FOR REFLECTION, DISCUSSION, AND PRAYER

How have you experienced the struggle of waiting and hope?

....

....

....

....

....

....

....

....

....

....

....

....

....

....

As you think about your community, your nation, and our world, where do you see that struggle now?

....

....

....

....

....

....

....

....

....

....

What other scriptures, songs, or poems might provide appropriate language for lament and hope in waiting?

....

....

....

....

....

....

....

....

....

....

TUESDAY

They Will Be Comforted

SCRIPTURE

MATTHEW 5:1–12

Blessed are the poor in spirit,
for theirs is the kingdom of heaven.
Blessed are those who mourn,
for they will be comforted.

—MATTHEW 5:3–4

In my experience there are few things more painful or disempowering than smiley platitudes in the midst of a long season of waiting. I've been through several of these seasons myself, but the most painful to date were the years of infertility and miscarriages before my first child was born. Month after month, optimism became more difficult, and the cheery words of others did less and less to encourage me.

It became increasingly difficult to put on a happy face, but I resisted my own grief and sought numerous ways to distract or numb myself: keeping busy and overcommitted, binge-watching British period dramas, giving myself as little time in silence as possible. But this avoidance only resulted in exhaustion and emotional detachment in all areas of my life. Finally I caved one day in my kitchen and had it all out with God. No longer able to keep the pain at bay, I voiced an angry, weepy lament of my current situation: how I longed to be a mother, how unfair it felt that I wasn't, how I didn't think I could keep waiting, even how guilty I felt for expressing all this negativity. (I was a pastor, after all! Shouldn't I be better at this hope thing?)

I didn't really know what to expect, but something remarkable happened in the moments that followed. I had a feeling of stillness and peace I had not known in a long, long time. I sensed God's presence not as a distant reality but as a very close friend. And while I was not given answers or sent an angel announcing my pregnancy, I was given a deep and abiding sense of God's compassion and goodness—which gave me hope. I had hope that I was seen and had not been forgotten. I had hope that God longed to give me good things because God loves me. I had hope that God was present and active in my life, even if I didn't know what God was doing.

In that moment I was not assured that I would become a mother. Although I begged for that promise, I didn't receive it. Instead, I was assured that God is good and faithful. Because of that, I could have hope for my future *even if* I did not become a mother in the way I wanted. I sank to the bottom of my reality and found that my true source of hope was not an eventual fulfillment of my desire to have a child but a God who does all things well.

What I experienced that day in my kitchen happened many more times over my roller-coaster ride of a journey to motherhood. Every time I had the courage to name my disappointment and express my suffering through lament, my hope was strengthened. Perhaps you've experienced this kind of mystifying hope in the midst of lament as well.

I've never actually been in a free-falling elevator, but I imagine this process to be like what being in a free-falling elevator might be like, everything in us resisting the impact at the bottom. All along the way we scramble to find something that will hold, grasping at quick fixes to suspend the fall momentarily before it resumes its descent with seemingly faster speed. The farther we fall, the more we realize none of our own solutions is enough to match the magnitude of the need.

Then, just when it seems that despair might have the last word, when all our human engineering has failed, we touch bottom. But, much to our relief, it's not the traumatic crash landing we expected. Instead, we find ourselves on nothing other than that solid ground we've been singing about all these years: *On Christ the Solid Rock I stand; all other ground is sinking sand!*

Lament reorients us to know the truth and hold unswervingly to the hope we profess that the One who promised *is* faithful (see Hebrews 10:23)! Perhaps this paradoxical hope paradox is the blessing Jesus promised to those who know the language of mourning and lament.

QUESTIONS FOR REFLECTION, DISCUSSION, AND PRAYER

When have you attempted to resist your own feelings of grief or disappointment? Why do you think humans do this?

....

....

....

....

....

....

....

....

....

....

....

When have you experienced the strengthening of your hope in the middle of lament?

....

....

....

....

....

....

....

....

....

....

....

What lament do you need to voice now in order for your hope to be strengthened?

....

....

....

....

....

....

....

....

....

....

Those Who Mourn

SCRIPTURE

ROMANS 12:9–21

*Be joyful in hope, patient in affliction, faithful in prayer.
Share with the Lord's people who are in need.
Practice hospitality.*

*Rejoice with those who rejoice;
mourn with those who mourn.*

—ROMANS 12:12–13, 15

The journey of waiting, hoping, and lamenting is not merely an individual enterprise. As people who embody the hope and love of Christ, we are united with all Christians praying, rejoicing, and mourning together. But if we can't make space for our own lament, we will struggle to join in the lament of others. And when we are unable to mourn with those who mourn, we risk doing harm to the body of Christ and the witness of the church.

Admittedly, U.S. Christians are not so good at practicing collective lament. Our music, our bestselling books, and our most popular sermon series reveal we are much more comfortable focusing on happy things. But if we have ears to hear, there are cries of lament going up all around us. Are we paying attention? Do we hear the cries of our brothers and sisters of color lamenting the ongoing destruction caused by racism in our nation? Do we hear the wailing of parents whose children have been lost to the steady uptick of gun violence? Can we listen to the pain a family carries due to their loved one's mental illness? Have we heard the lament of the single mom desperately trying to keep her family together?

Many of us struggle to enter the deep grief of others because we have no idea how to fix the problems that cause the grief. But when we study Lamentations and the psalms of lament, we realize those who practice lament are not looking for quick fixes or immediate answers. It is completely counterintuitive in our high-achieving, results-driven culture, but lament is not focused on *fixing* the problem; it is focused on correctly *naming* the problem. In lament we confess to the truth, fully agreeing with God and one another about the way things are: no masks, no hiding, no whitewashing over the ugly spots.

The very same coin holds the other side of the truth: when we agree with God on all that is *wrong*, we are invited to join God in seeing, waiting on, and working toward what is *right*. In our waiting, we become more convinced than ever that we do need saving—not only as individuals but also as the whole collective of creation and humanity. And we are equally convinced that there is only One who can do it. Our collective pain will not be assuaged by anything less than God's way of justice, peace, healing, and freedom. Our lament becomes a prayer of words and deeds: *May your kingdom come and your will be done on earth as it is in heaven!*

Sometimes mourning with those who mourn does look like showing up to the hospital and weeping alongside someone. I have received the healing power of this gift, and I hope you have too. Other times it means listening to a person whose life experiences are totally different from your own, while acknowledging that their pain and grief are worth your attention. It might look like watching the news through the lens of love and praying with or at least for the individuals whose pain makes the headlines. Sometimes it looks like going out of your way to sit with the newly divorced woman at church instead of letting her sit alone.

In joining the weeping lament of others, we give witness to a grand and glorious hope that is far greater than merely putting on a happy face.

When we choose to weep with someone whose pain doesn't have to affect our lives, we showcase the light and love of Christ that are present with us even in the darkest places. When we show up in another's painful season of waiting, their struggle becomes ours, and ours become theirs, and the hope of Christ is strengthened in us both.

QUESTIONS FOR REFLECTION, DISCUSSION, AND PRAYER

When has someone mourned with you when you were mourning?

....

....

....

....

....

....

....

....

....

....

....

....

....

....

Who is lamenting around you—whether locally, nationally, or globally?

....

....

....

....

....

....

....

....

....

....

....

How is God inviting you to join in the lament of others right now?

....

....

....

....

....

....

....

....

....

....

THURSDAY

SCRIPTURE

LUKE 13:31–35

Jerusalem, Jerusalem, killer of prophets, abuser of the messengers of God! How often I've longed to gather your children, gather your children like a hen, her brood safe under her wings—but you refused and turned away!

—LUKE 13:34 (MSG)

We might not be accustomed to thinking of God as lamenting, but Jesus teaches us that God can and does lament. Near the end of his ministry, Jesus picks up a familiar refrain of lament voiced by generations of Israel's prophets. Hosea, Isaiah, Jeremiah, and Ezekiel are among those who were taught to sing the lament song of God's own heart:

How long, oh my people?! How long will you run from me when I call you? (see Hosea 11:2).

How long will you deny the severity of your wounds and claim "peace" when there is no peace? (see Jeremiah 8:11).

If only you would let me lead you, if only you would let me care for you as a shepherd cares for the sheep (see Ezekiel 34:11).

If only you would be my people and let me be your God—no longer would there be violence in your land, and I would provide you with everlasting light (see Isaiah 60).

The sad history of Israel is the result of these words falling on deaf ears. The prophets lamented the reality that the people of Israel could not or did not want to see. Instead they preferred the messages of false prophets who promised prosperity and peace—no repentance necessary. It is an unfortunate and deadly trend that has continued to plague the people of God: we silence and kill the very messengers who bring the message we need the most.

That is why Jesus laments. He cries out as a parent in pain, watching beloved children choose destruction. Jesus laments for a people who are so confident they know what is right for themselves that they refuse the embrace of their loving parent. These words of Jesus in today's scripture are troubling and painful. But woven within this lament of a desire yet to be fulfilled is the beauty of that desire itself.

Mother hens gather their chicks under their wings as a protective measure against threats, using their own bodies to shield their young. This image is full of tenderness, fierceness, and self-sacrificing love—and it's the best way Jesus knows to describe the longing of his own heart. Jesus reveals that God's greatest desire is to be like a Good Mother to us, surrounding us with wings of protection, nurture, and love.

This image is such an extravagant picture of love that it can feel hard to believe, even harder to accept. Perhaps that's why God has been waiting so long, ready to gather us if only we allow it. This is a God who knows what it is like to suffer the pain of waiting. God has waited for all of human history for God's children to let themselves be loved!

What if God didn't have to wait anymore? What if we *did* let Jesus gather us? How would things be if God's hope were realized, and how do we get there? It seems we would have to start by admitting there is real danger and turmoil surrounding us and that we do, in fact, need the protective shelter God offers us. It would require coming to God with our honesty—our hopes, fears, needs, longings, laments, and all—instead of trying to pretend that we're doing fine all on our own. We would have to commit to stop stiff-arming the One who loves us and learn how to surrender. In short, I think it looks like giving God room and time to show us what God's love feels like.

If God were to really get the desires of God's own heart, it would not be an individual experience. As we allow ourselves to be gathered, we join a whole host of others being gathered up too. We would be all squished up together in the group hug of God's heart, where we find ourselves part of a much larger family than we ever could have imagined! Then the rest of our lives could be lived from this place of belonging, security, and love.

According to Jesus, *God's* hope is that we know how dearly loved we are and that we let that love change everything. And *our* hope is found in this God whose love is greater than we can comprehend, whose love does indeed change everything. Thanks be to God.

QUESTIONS FOR REFLECTION, DISCUSSION, AND PRAYER

What stirs in you as you think of God waiting, hoping, and lamenting?

....

....

....

....

....

....

....

....

....

What places can you identify within yourself that resist being gathered under God's wings?

....

....

....

....

....

....

....

....

....

....

....

How do you want to respond to Jesus's lament?

....

....

....

....

....

....

....

....

....

....

....

FRIDAY

Rest & Reflect

Look back at the readings from this week. Which scripture, idea, or story stands out to you as most meaningful or most challenging? Take time to revisit it and listen for the Spirit's invitation to go deeper.

What have you learned about yourself and/or about God as you've practiced lament this week?

....

....

....

....

....

....

....

....

....

....

....

....

How has hope taken shape within you this week?

....
....
....
....
....
....
....
....
....
....
....

What practices or ideas from this week do you want to take with you as regular practices for your life?

....
....
....
....
....
....
....
....
....
....

DECEMBER 8, 2024

Praise be to the Lord, the God of Israel,
because he has come to his people and redeemed them.
He has raised up a horn of salvation for us
in the house of his servant David
(as he said through his holy prophets of long ago),
salvation from our enemies
and from the hand of all who hate us—
to show mercy to our ancestors
and to remember his holy covenant,
the oath he swore to our father Abraham:
to rescue us from the hand of our enemies,
and to enable us to serve him without fear
in holiness and righteousness before him all our days.

—LUKE 1:68–75

Hope points to love because the assurance of love at work makes it possible to hope in the first place. In this second week of Advent, we are invited to think on the love of God that is unlike anything else in creation. We use the English word "love" a lot. We love our family or closest friends, but we can also love tacos, a particular color, and our favorite sports teams. There's only one English word for all of it. But the love of God throughout the Old and New Testament is talked about in very particular language that is not used for anything else.

The Hebrew word *chesed* and the Greek word *agape* are used to talk about the holy, unique love of God that is more like a never-ending commitment than a feeling of affection. Neither word describes action born from duty-bound obligation or resentment. The commitment of *chesed* or *agape* love is not mandated by any outside force. Instead it is driven by a selflessness that leads the one who loves to voluntarily do what no one has a right to expect or ask.

Today's scripture speaks of the never-ending love of God at work. Zechariah and Elizabeth spent decades longing for a child while experiencing the grief of infertility. Then one day, while he worked in the temple, Zechariah received a visit from the angel Gabriel to tell him he would have a son who would help fulfill God's plan to redeem Israel. Zechariah was so filled with unbelief that he was unable to speak for the whole of Elizabeth's pregnancy. Nine long months of silence later, Zechariah finally regained his ability to speak, and the words in today's scripture are the first ones he says.

Zechariah's song of praise has little to do with his and Elizabeth's personal experience of waiting for a child. Instead, his attention is on the even longer period of waiting that has been endured by all of Abraham's descendants. Zechariah sees his own life and his son's birth through the lens of history, recognizing the through-line of God's faithful, steadfast love. His story is continued proof of the hope voiced in the midst of deepest grief by those lamenting Jerusalem's destruction centuries earlier: "The steadfast love of the LORD never ceases, his mercies never come to an end; they are new every morning; great is your faithfulness. 'The LORD is my portion,' says my soul, 'therefore I will hope in him'" (Lamentations 3:22–24, NRSVUE).

This kind of love is not something one can understand or acknowledge cognitively. It is incomprehensible. It is a love we can only fully know within relationship—both in our own lives and through the stories of those who came before us. This is the *chesed, agape* love that we are invited to experience, receive, and share during this second week of Advent.

QUESTIONS FOR REFLECTION, DISCUSSION, AND PRAYER

Based on the descriptions of *chesed* and *agape* set against your own experiences, how would you define God's love?

....

....

....

....

....

....

....

....

....

....

....

....

....

....

....

....

....

....

....

....

What examples of God's *chesed, agape* love come to mind from Scripture, stories from the tradition of the universal church, or from your own life?

....

....

....

....

....

....

....

....

....

....

....

....

....

....

....

....

....

....

....

....

....

Which is easier: to learn *about* love, or to open ourselves up to *experience* love? Why?

....

....

....

....

....

....

....

....

....

....

....

....

....

....

....

....

....

....

....

....

....

....

....

....

....

....

His Unfailing Love

SCRIPTURE

PSALM 107

Give thanks to the Lord, for he is good;
his love endures forever.

Let the redeemed of the Lord tell their story—
those he redeemed from the hand of the foe,
those he gathered from the lands,
from east and west, from north and south.

Let them give thanks to the Lord for his unfailing love
and his wonderful deeds for mankind,
for he satisfies the thirsty
and fills the hungry with good things.

—PSALM 107:1–3, 8–9

Psalm 107 offers a litany of ways God has extended unfailing love to God's beloved ones awaiting rescue. Some were wandering in wastelands (v. 4); others were sitting in deepest gloom (v. 10); some suffered the pain of foolish decisions (v. 17); still more were in the middle of a storm (vv. 25–26). No matter the circumstance, the steadfast love of the Lord reached them. And each one is a story worthy to be told.

Every story of rescue and redemption is unique, whether in Scripture or our own lives. But all of these unique stories are part of our collective history as people who have been redeemed by the Lord's unfailing love. And no one person's story remains a singular story. Everyone who has known the redeeming love of God becomes a conduit of God's love for others. The ripple effects extend throughout all time and all across the globe. I am writing this, and you are reading this, as part of a long chain reaction of God's loving activity throughout history.

None of us can know all the stories of redemption that make up our biological or faith lineage. But one of the stories I am grateful to know is that of my great-great-grandmother, Erika "Mor-Mor" Boquist. She was born in Sweden in 1857, to parents who were not married. In that culture and time, having children out of wedlock was considered an egregious scandal, one that typically doomed the children in question to a shame-filled, impoverished future. But thanks be to God, her life was marked by God's redeeming grace rather than the limitations of her culture.

While I don't know the details of how she encountered God's love, it is clear that she did, and she dedicated her life to sharing God's love with others. She eventually became a mother of six who served alongside her pastor husband, Karl. He led a church-renewal movement that faced severe persecution, which led the family to emigrate from their home and go to the United States. They continued to serve and lead faithfully in Minnesota, caring for many as Karl preached, planted new churches, and became a founding leader of the Swedish Covenant denomination.

Several years ago, my father received a large collection of family papers that included the will Erika personally wrote several years before her death. She had few possessions. Instead, she shared about God's faithfulness and her fervent desire for all her children and their children to know the love of God. Her will is in actuality a written prayer, evidence of the many prayers prayed and answered through her whole life. It is an incredibly humbling and holy thing to read these century-old words and recognize my own story in the ripple effects of hers.

Not all of us can trace the story of God's love back through our biological lineage. But we all have someone—whether a Sunday school teacher, pastor, friend, neighbor, foster parent, mentor, or someone else—whose own redemption story made way for our own. Who are those people for you? Do you know the story of God's love in their lives? If you don't and are able to connect with them, consider reaching out to ask about it. Every story tells of the steadfast love of God and magnifies our understanding of just how true it is that this love endures *forever*.

QUESTIONS FOR REFLECTION, DISCUSSION, AND PRAYER

What is your own story of God's steadfast love? How and with whom are you telling that story?

....

....

....

....

....

....

....

....

....

....

....

Who are some of the people who have been a conduit of
God's redeeming love for you?

....

....

....

....

....

....

....

....

....

....

How do you experience God's love as you trace it through
the stories of those before you?

....

....

....

....

....

....

....

....

....

....

....

TUESDAY

You Are with Me

SCRIPTURE

PSALM 23

The Lord is my shepherd; I shall not want.
He makes me lie down in green pastures;
he leads me beside still waters;
he restores my soul.
He leads me in right paths
for his name's sake.

Even though I walk through the darkest valley,
I fear no evil;
for you are with me;
your rod and your staff,
they comfort me.

You prepare a table before me
in the presence of my enemies;
you anoint my head with oil;
my cup overflows.
Surely goodness and mercy shall follow me
all the days of my life,
and I shall dwell in the house of the Lord
my whole life long.

—PSALM 23 (NRSVUE)

Several years ago I read a quote from Carmelite nun and spiritual writer Ruth Burrows that dramatically altered the way I engage with God. She described God's love as something that was always at work giving God-self to us. We didn't have to work hard to entertain, pacify, or reach God to be loved. Instead, she said, if we truly understand who God is and what God is about, then our work is simply "to let ourselves be loved, let ourselves be given to, let ourselves be worked upon by this great God."[1] It sounds so beautiful. But practically speaking, how do we *let* ourselves be loved? How do we take on a posture of humble receptivity when we are so used to producing and performing?

The metaphor we are given of God as our shepherd is a helpful place to begin. Especially in our seasons of waiting when things are not moving as fast as we'd like, it is challenging to put ourselves in the position of the sheep instead of assuming the role of the shepherd. It requires submission, acknowledging that we need to be led and cared for. When Jesus called himself the Good Shepherd (John 10), he was calling on the imagery of Psalm 23 and inviting us to know his love in this very particular way.

When I enter Psalm 23 imagining Jesus as my shepherd, the first thing I'm confronted with is my difficulty to believe I have all I need. Usually I am surrounded by people and businesses reminding me of everything I *don't* have. What would it be like to be with a person whose very presence assured me I have enough? When I trust this truth, there is a settled peace that feels really good.

I imagine myself having a great time meandering the Galilean hillsides with Jesus—until he tells me it's time to take a nap. Then I feel my inner rebellious toddler rise up, indignant at the suggestion that he knows what I need better than I do. But when I finally give in and flop down, I realize he's right. I've been so used to living life in the rapids that walking along the quiet streams takes some getting used to. But now that I'm here, my tiredness kicks in. I have to admit, I can do a great job keeping

---

1. Ruth Burrows, *The Essence of Prayer* (Mahwah, NJ: Paulist Press, 2006), 176.

myself busy, productive, distracted, or entertained—but he is the only one who knows how to restore my soul.

The tools of the trade—a shepherd's rod and staff—don't sound all that comforting at first. But then I realize how he uses them, gently prodding and guiding me in the paths he knows are right. Even when I can't see his face, I know he's there. It is a huge relief to know I'm not alone, that I don't have to figure out my own route. I wish he would lead us *around* the dark valleys of fear and death instead of *through* them, but he doesn't. What he does do is stay with me so I don't go through them alone.

When we arrive at a place surrounded by those who want to do me harm, I look at Jesus in alarm: *where have you brought me?!* And I notice it's here he's decided to unpack the picnic basket. He prepares a feast for me, right in the midst of danger, and I am not harmed. His love and favor wash over me, and I am deeply aware that nothing could ever separate me from his love. These gifts of mercy and goodness will go with me everywhere, for the rest of my life, because my Good Shepherd is with me always.

QUESTIONS FOR REFLECTION, DISCUSSION, AND PRAYER

How do you respond to the idea that our task is to let ourselves be loved? What habits help you take this posture or keep you from it?

....

....

....

....

....

....

What is it like to imagine Jesus as your Good Shepherd?

....

....

....

....

....

....

....

....

....

Where do you need the loving care of your Good Shepherd today?

....

....

....

....

....

....

....

....

....

....

....

....

....

He Loved Them to the End

SCRIPTURE

JOHN 13:1–17

It was just before the Passover Festival. Jesus knew that the hour had come for him to leave this world and go to the Father. Having loved his own who were in the world, he loved them to the end.

So he got up from the meal, took off his outer clothing, and wrapped a towel around his waist. After that, he poured water into a basin and began to wash his disciples' feet, drying them with the towel that was wrapped around him.

"No," said Peter, "you shall never wash my feet."

Jesus answered, "Unless I wash you, you have no part with me."

—JOHN 13:1, 4–5, 8

This story may seem out of place in Advent, but it has a lot to say to us as we wait. The disciples around this Passover table were also waiting for God to act. In fact, all the Jewish people were waiting for the promised Messiah to overpower the Romans and make Israel great again. Now, after the triumphal entry and the rising fury of the religious leaders, the disciples just knew something big was about to happen.

With everyone around Jesus waiting for him to instigate some cataclysmic event, Jesus gets up from the table and—washes their feet? They were waiting for Jesus to do something big and glorious, and this was shockingly small and dirty. Here, in the midst of a group waiting for a king to show up, Jesus provides the clearest picture of who our King is and what our King does.

Many of us, like the disciples, are eager for God to get to work "out there," fixing all that is wrong in the world. In the darkness of our Advent waiting, we long for God to bring an end to the injustice, deception, suffering, and evil that run rampant in our world. We dream of the day God will vanquish our enemies in a big way. But what if, while we wait for God to get to work out there, Jesus decides to show up in here, right at our very feet, with a towel and a basin? Or maybe, for those of us who are not accustomed to foot-washing, Jesus shows up to scrub our bathroom, clean out our storage unit, or tackle that pile of dishes in the sink. Whatever the metaphor, we are given an image of Jesus voluntarily stooping down into the muck of our lives to care for us in the places we're too embarrassed to let anyone else touch.

Sometimes I think it would be easier if Jesus were only interested in the big picture. The way he wants to talk about and touch on such deeply personal things feels intimidating and even risky. I am ready to show Jesus how good I am at serving people—but he asks if I'm ready to let him serve me. I'm good at pointing out what those people need over there, but he asks what I want him to do for *me*. I want Jesus to go out and heal the world—but he asks me to show him my wounds, my grief, my disappointment.

This whole being-loved-to-the-end thing requires a lot of us. And when we are tempted to balk at his outrageous request to enter into the dirtiest details of our lives, we are reminded of his response to Peter, which is essentially, "Well, it's this or nothing." In loving us to the end, Jesus invites us to let him into the very end of *ourselves*—so that nothing is left untouched or hidden away. It isn't easy to open ourselves up like that. It requires courage, vulnerability, and humility. And it is deeply *good*.

So what happens if we're just not ready yet to let Jesus into the muck? Perhaps the very best news of all is that this is not only a once-in-a-life-time opportunity. The steadfast love of the Lord is new *every* morning. Jesus is ready whenever we are.

QUESTIONS FOR REFLECTION, DISCUSSION, AND PRAYER

Do you find it easier to imagine God acting in great power "out there," or in loving service "in here"?

....

....

....

....

....

....

....

....

....

....

....

....

How does it feel to think of Jesus stooping down to serve you?

....
....
....
....
....
....
....
....
....

How is God asking you to let yourself be loved today?

....
....
....
....
....
....
....
....
....
....
....
....
....

Come Have Breakfast

SCRIPTURE

JOHN 21:1–14

*When they landed, they saw a fire of burning coals
there with fish on it, and some bread.*

*Jesus said to them, "Bring some of the fish you have just
caught." So Simon Peter climbed back into the boat and
dragged the net ashore. It was full of large fish, 153, but even
with so many the net was not torn. Jesus said to them,
"Come and have breakfast." None of the disciples dared
ask him, "Who are you?" They knew it was the Lord.
Jesus came, took the bread and gave it to them,
and did the same with the fish. This was now
the third time Jesus appeared to his disciples
after he was raised from the dead.*

—*JOHN 21:9–14*

Because this is a story we usually visit in the season of Easter, it can be easy to forget that the disciples were in a new and disorienting liminal space. *We* know they were between the resurrection and Jesus's ascension and that Pentecost was soon to follow. But *they* didn't know that.

All they knew was that they had been recruited by Jesus to be fishers of people, but then that whole thing didn't go where they thought it would, and now in the aftermath of crucifixion and resurrection, they were trying to figure out what to do with their lives. So they returned to what they knew best—fishing for fish instead of people. But even that wasn't normal, and a fruitless night on the lake turned into a miraculous catch of fish and breakfast on the beach with Jesus.

Have you ever been so thoroughly confused by a situation that you don't even know what questions to ask? I imagine that was the state these disciples were in. If it were me, I would have been ready for Jesus to show up and explain a *lot*. But Jesus knows the loving response is not always giving us what we *want* but giving us what we truly *need*. After an exhausting night of no sleep and no fish, they didn't need more information. They needed breakfast. I think I can relate.

Several years ago, I was given the gift of a sabbatical. Within the span of four years I had two babies and planted a church. I was tired. I began my sabbatical on retreat, where I was encouraged to spend time in prayer with this story in John 21. I felt myself gravitating toward the end, where Jesus invites Peter to feed his sheep, because I had long identified that as part of my own calling as a pastor and a mom. But I was also pretty worn out from feeding people—parishioners and toddlers alike. I felt myself leaning toward resentment at the thought that God had led me on sabbatical to give me more work to do.

When I read the story again, a lightbulb turned on as I realized I had jumped ahead in the story. Before Jesus asks Peter to feed anyone, Jesus feeds *Peter*! Before Jesus includes Peter in his work of shepherding, he is a Good Shepherd *to* Peter. And in that moment of my own exhaustion, I recognized Jesus showing up to offer *me* what I needed most—not a lot of answers, and certainly not a task list, but nourishment for my soul.

Jesus is not just the Good Shepherd for Peter, pastors, and mothers. He is the Good Shepherd for *all* of us, which includes you. Jesus knows how to find you on your own beach of exhaustion, confusion, and discouragement. Jesus knows how to say your name, and he knows what you need most. Jesus knows how you like your breakfast, and he's already prepared it for you. Take a moment now and imagine the place where

Jesus meets you and the meal he's made for you. Let yourself be loved by your Good Shepherd, and return as often as you need.

QUESTIONS FOR REFLECTION, DISCUSSION, AND PRAYER

How have you experienced food as an expression of love?

....

....

....

....

....

....

....

....

....

....

....

....

....

....

....

....

....

....

What image comes to mind when you think of Jesus as your
breakfast maker?

....
....
....
....
....
....
....
....
....

What do you find most comforting or most challenging about
letting Jesus love you this way?

....
....
....
....
....
....
....
....
....
....
....
....
....

FRIDAY

Rest & Reflect

Look back at the readings from this week. Which scripture, idea, or story stands out to you as most meaningful or most challenging? Take time to revisit it and listen for the Spirit's invitation to go deeper.

What have you learned about yourself and/or about God this week?

....

....

....

....

....

....

....

....

....

....

....

....

....

How have you responded to the invitation to let yourself be loved?

....
....
....
....
....
....
....
....
....
....

What practices or ideas from this week do you want to take with you as regular practices for your life?

....
....
....
....
....
....
....
....
....
....
....

DECEMBER 15, 2024

SCRIPTURE

ISAIAH 12:2-6

Surely God is my salvation;
I will trust and will not be afraid,
for the LORD is my strength and my might;
he has become my salvation.
With joy you will draw water from the wells of salvation.

Shout aloud and sing for joy, O royal Zion,
for great in your midst is the Holy One of Israel.

—ISAIAH 12:2-3, 6 (NRSVUE)

Joy seems to be much more a Christmas thing than an Advent thing. We associate joy with the sense of relief, accomplishment, and finality that are so emblematic of Jesus's birth story. The wait of pregnancy and the suffering of labor are over, and a tiny baby has arrived. Joy to the world, indeed!

But here in the third week of Advent we are introduced to another form of joy that is not dependent on a specific outcome. This joy is the surprising gift that shows up in the midst of all that is yet to be completed. As a hallmark of God's kingdom, joy is not only the promise of what's to come, but it's also a reality that is available and present *now*. This experience of joy is not only unexpected; it is even subversive. We know "joy comes with the morning" (Psalm 30:5, NRSVUE), but who would expect to experience joy in the dark of night, while the sunrise is still such a long way off?

In our times of waiting, like Advent, we become acutely aware of what is wrong in our world and how desperately we need a Savior. But if we only see all that is wrong, we have already succumbed to the oppressive forces of death and despair. The reality of God's kingdom bears witness to the fact that there is more going on in the world than the work of death. Joy itself is resistance to the principalities and powers that are constantly at work to steal, kill, and destroy all signs of life. This is because joy doesn't wait until everything gets better to make its appearance. Joy is defiant, subversive, and persistent. Like wildflowers finding their way through the cracks of asphalt, or pinpricks of light shining through the darkness, the joy of God cannot be shut out!

But please hear me—this is in no way the same thing as putting on a happy face. Joy cannot be faked or manufactured. It doesn't show up by ignoring all that is wrong or distracting ourselves with something fun while we wait it out. It is truly the fruit of the Spirit, growing wherever there is space and time for the Spirit to do its work. Like all fruit, joy is something we can either squash or nurture. It is the Spirit's fruit, but the soil in which it grows is ours. So if we cannot muster it up on our own, how do we experience this surprising, subversive gift of God's joy? How can we learn to see the joy that comes *before* the morning?

Like all things worth doing, it requires intentionality and practice. Joy comes naturally as a result of being given good gifts. If we're not used to seeing them, it can take effort to recognize and name the gifts we've been given. But once we know what we're looking for, we start seeing gifts everywhere! We call the practice of naming gifts *gratitude*, and it is an indispensable tool in cultivating joy. Throughout this third week of Advent we will practice gratitude, naming the good gifts around us and making space for God's joy to flourish.

A gift is anything good that you did not create or make happen for yourself. It can be anything—from your favorite ice cream, to the smile on your kid's face, to the beauty of a flower or an energizing conversation. Because we live in a world that God created, and live in relationship with other humans who help supply everything we use and eat, there are few things we can take sole credit for. Even things you purchase can count as gifts because there is a long chain reaction of other people's work, creativity, and our own opportunities that we did not make happen.

Throughout this week, look for the gifts in your life with a goal in mind of listing one hundred gifts before the end of the week. Each of this week's readings may help you notice the gifts that come in different shapes and sizes.

QUESTIONS FOR REFLECTION, DISCUSSION, AND PRAYER

What brings you joy?

....

....

....

....

....

....

....

....

....

....

....

....

....

....

....

....

....

....

....

....

....

How have you noticed the two kinds of joy at work in your life—the joy of completion and the joy that comes while things are still in progress?

....

....

....

....

....

....

....

....

....

....

....

....

....

....

....

....

....

....

....

....

....

Is it commonplace or challenging for you to notice and name gifts in your life?

....

....

....

....

....

....

....

....

....

....

....

....

....

....

....

....

....

....

....

....

....

....

....

....

Their Voice Goes Out

SCRIPTURE

PSALM 19

The heavens declare the glory of God;
the skies proclaim the work of his hands.
Day after day they pour forth speech;
night after night they reveal knowledge.
They have no speech, they use no words;
no sound is heard from them.
Yet their voice goes out into all the earth,
their words to the ends of the world.

—PSALM 19:1–4A

In our busy, technology-dependent, twenty-first-century lives, we are prone to overlook some of the very best gifts we've been given in creation. The intricate details, colors, variety, and beauty found in God's good creation are there for us to enjoy. This world was not created by some great pragmatist who only cared about efficiency. The world we live in declares the glory of God in the minutia of a hummingbird, the stunning diversity of the ocean, the mysteries of the stars, and the miracle of the seasons.

Recently a friend told me she had discovered a new pastime in bird watching. She was shy in admitting she had purchased a bird feeder for her backyard and gave time every day to watching them gather around it. Not too long ago she would have considered this a silly waste of time, something altogether unproductive. Yet this simple act has become a regular bright spot in her day and, much to her surprise, even a necessary spiritual practice. Watching the birds swoop, play, and gather while they sing, she said, brings her joy. It refocuses her attention from the details of her own life to the intricacies of the larger creation to which she belongs.

My friend is not alone. Recent studies have proven there are significant mental health benefits to spending time in nature and specifically hearing birdsong. It is especially effective in providing relief to those suffering from depression.[1] While these scientific studies are certainly not making spiritual claims, they provide reminders of what Scripture and the saints have been saying all along. There is a Creator who made all that is around us and called it *good*. Then this Creator put us humans right in the middle of it, giving it all to us not just as pragmatic resources but also as superfluous beauty to be *enjoyed*.

Admittedly, some of us have an easier time in nature than others. For those who live in large cities or have limited mobility, it's more common to be surrounded by the handiwork of humans than God's in nature. But we don't have to be exposed to great expanses of wilderness to find joy in creation. If we slow down long enough to notice, we can be moved to wonder and joy through the intricacies of a flower in the park, trees changing in the seasons, a potted plant stretching to the light of our window, or the rapid accumulation of a billion tiny snowflakes as we watch from indoors.

The good gifts of God's creation bring joy because they remind us of many truths. The world is so much bigger than us. This remembrance brings a kind of joyful humility so we can take our place in the beloved creation as created ones and receive the good news that we are not God. When we spend time listening to the song creation sings, we find there

1. Ryan Hammoud, Stefania Tognin, Lucie Burgess, et al., "Smartphone-based Ecological Momentary Assessment Reveals Mental Health Benefits of Birdlife, *Scientific Reports* 12, #17589 (2022), https://doi.org/10.1038/s41598-022-20207-6.

is waiting built into everything. Nothing in the natural world changes instantly. Each season and each change has its own process and its own gifts. Perhaps God's good creation can teach us to trust that this is true for ourselves as well.

QUESTIONS FOR REFLECTION, DISCUSSION, AND PRAYER

How often do you spend time enjoying creation?

....

....

....

....

....

....

....

....

....

....

....

....

....

....

....

....

What good gifts of nature are available to you now?

....
....
....
....
....
....
....
....
....
....

What gifts in your past or present are you noticing today?

....
....
....
....
....
....
....
....
....
....
....
....

You Will Go Out in Joy

SCRIPTURE

ISAIAH 55

Come, all you who are thirsty,
come to the waters;
and you who have no money,
come, buy and eat!
Come, buy wine and milk
without money and without cost.
Why spend money on what is not bread,
and your labor on what does not satisfy?
Listen, listen to me, and eat what is good,
and you will delight in the richest of fare.

You will go out in joy
and be led forth in peace;
the mountains and hills
will burst into song before you,
and all the trees of the field
will clap their hands.

—ISAIAH 55:1–3, 12

Early in our marriage, my husband and I spent a year of volunteer missionary service in the small southern African nation of Eswatini (then Swaziland). Much of our work was in response to the HIV/AIDS epidemic, and one of our first tasks was to help organize a container shipment of medical supplies from a group of donors in the U.S. Because the container itself was also being gifted as additional hospital storage, we needed to hire a crane to lift it off the truck. Now that high-speed internet and Google have found their way to Eswatini, this task may not be so hard today. But back then, I quickly learned it was going to be much harder than I ever anticipated to get what was needed on the exact day we needed it.

The day before the shipment was to arrive, we were still scrambling. I had called, left messages, and had many conversations that barely broke through language barriers. Still there was no crane. With the shipment under twenty-four hours away, the pressure was mounting, and I had exhausted everything I knew to do. After crying exasperated tears, I decided to take a nap and hoped I would have new energy to think of something else when I woke up.

An hour later, I woke to my phone ringing. It was a call from someone who heard what I was looking for, and they asked if I still needed help. While they did not have a crane, there was a large forklift they assured me could do the job! I admit, I was skeptical, but I was also immediately flooded with relief and joy. The work was not complete, but my joy in that moment was not about being finished. It was about the realization that God had been at work—*while I took a nap!* And, incidentally, the forklift did work, which brought more joy later!

My husband and I have returned to this story many times to draw on its truth. But it's not true only for us—it's a universal truth that says much more about who God is than anything else. There are times when all of us have tried everything we know to do and have still come up short. We have exhausted ourselves with seemingly nothing to show for it, arriving empty-handed, frustrated, maybe even ashamed. Then God shows up and provides what we couldn't, filling our empty hands with what is good—whether it's what we've been asking for or something else entirely. There are many times I've thrown up my hands, taken a nap, and woken up without the thing being fixed but with a new sense of peace in place of my anxiety.

The joyful truth here is not that we always get what we want but that we have a God who is working on our behalf with resources we can't comprehend. This is an invitation into a whole new reality of *abundance* that gives us permission to *rest*. It is not all up to us to get what we need or to fulfill what others need. In the reality of God's kingdom, there is more at work in the world than what we make happen ourselves. And this is very good news! This is reason for joy, indeed.

The reality of abundance and rest in God's kingdom is available to us always, but it usually takes us coming to the end of our own resources to realize it—which is perhaps why the gift of joy surprises us so much in our waiting. When we don't have what we need, longing for what is yet to come, our capacity for accepting God's abundant provision expands. In this upturned landscape, we can name our empty-handedness as a gift that allows us to be filled by God, leading us to go out in joy.

QUESTIONS FOR REFLECTION, DISCUSSION, AND PRAYER

How have you encountered God's abundance in providing what you couldn't make happen?

....

....

....

....

....

....

....

....

When have you experienced the joy of receiving rest before the work was done?

....
....
....
....
....
....
....
....
....
....

What changes within yourself have you noticed as you've been naming gifts this week?

....
....
....
....
....
....
....
....
....
....

WEDNESDAY

A Remote Place

SCRIPTURE

MATTHEW 14:13-21

As evening approached, the disciples came to him and said, "This is a remote place, and it's already getting late. Send the crowds away, so they can go to the villages and buy themselves some food."

Jesus replied, "They do not need to go away. You give them something to eat."

—MATTHEW 14:15-16

It seems God reserves some of God's best work for the remote places. Time and time again, deserts and wildernesses are the backdrop for the most surprising of God's gifts. Like the newly freed Israelites who received daily manna in the desert, the thousands who followed Jesus into this remote place did not need to leave it in order to be well fed. When we travel with the Good Shepherd, the wilderness can be a surprising source of joy for us as well.

In March 2020, the whole world was plunged deep into wilderness as COVID lockdowns began and life as we knew it ground to a halt. We were far removed from our day-to-day routines, from our ability to gather, and from our sense of certainty and well-being. And all this was accompanied by suffering and grief for those who experienced the reality of the illness and the death it too often brought. It was indeed a time of darkness and waiting, with very little knowledge of when it would ever get better.

The congregation I was pastoring at the time in Oklahoma City had a habit of taking on one practice a week to live out what we heard in Sunday's sermon. Following the saddest Easter service I've ever experienced, in which we all huddled around screens in our own living spaces and watched a pre-recorded service preached to an empty room, we pastors invited people into a practice of looking for signs of life. The resurrection, we said, means that death does not get the last word. So even in the midst of ongoing lockdowns, rising death tolls, and the crippling effects of isolation, we were determined to find signs of new life and joy somewhere, somehow.

We created a way for people to share their findings on social media so we could see and be encouraged by one another's experiences. Thanks be to God, we began to find what we were looking for. In fact, we found so much that we quickly realized one week of this practice was not enough, so we kept it up all through the seven-week season of Easter. In those weeks our congregation learned to see and celebrate gifts in all kinds of unexpected places: wildflowers in bloom, handwritten notes, weekday bike rides on empty streets, everlasting sourdough starter, shared packages of toilet paper, school lunches prepared and delivered, sidewalk chalk messages left for passersby. Some of the gifts we found were there all along—we'd just been too busy to notice.

But the most surprising gifts were those that were specific to the COVID-imposed wilderness. At a time when it would have been easy to think only of one's own needs, every creative act to care for another was worthy of celebration. People picked up medication and dropped it off on porches; others made deliveries of food and care packages; some donated their government stimulus checks to those who had lost jobs; many wrote notes of encouragement to healthcare professionals. By lamenting together the suffering and injustice of the pandemic, we found ways to offer and receive hope. Together we experienced the most unexpected and subversive kind of joy in the very same places as our grief.

The joy we found did not make our waiting go faster or our wilderness less present. But it did sustain us and empower us to move differently in it. We cannot deny that the isolation and loss of the pandemic have marked us all forever. But in that little community our shared, surprising encounters with joy also shaped us in beautiful ways. This happens to all of us in the wilderness, I think. The gifts we are given in these most remote places do more than fill our bellies. They broaden our expectations and teach us to be open to the possibility of joy, even in the places we'd least like to be.

QUESTIONS FOR REFLECTION, DISCUSSION, AND PRAYER

What surprising gifts can you identify that have brought joy in the remote places of your own life?

....

....

....

....

....

....

....

....

....

....

Where do you need to ask for the Spirit's help to recognize good gifts even in the wilderness?

....

....

....

....

....

....

....

....

....

....

What gifts from your past or present are you noticing today?

....

....

....

....

....

....

....

....

....

....

....

Fixing Our Eyes on Jesus

SCRIPTURE

HEBREWS 12

Therefore, since we are surrounded by such a great cloud of witnesses, let us throw off everything that hinders and the sin that so easily entangles. And let us run with perseverance the race marked out for us, fixing our eyes on Jesus, the pioneer and perfecter of faith. For the joy set before him he endured the cross, scorning its shame, and sat down at the right hand of the throne of God. Consider him who endured such opposition from sinners, so that you will not grow weary and lose heart.

—HEBREWS 12:1–3

A preacher once gave an illustration of life with God that I've returned to often. Sometimes, he said, we have this idea that God is behind us or somewhere overhead, shouting at us to walk forward in obedience. But the better image, he said, is that of God as a parent teaching a toddler how to walk. The parent stands out in front of the toddler, beckoning with a smile, welcoming the child into the good future. This is the picture I have when the writer of Hebrews urges us to fix our eyes on Jesus. Perhaps this is even the picture of what Jesus was doing when he fixed his eyes on the "joy set before him."

After my long season of waiting to be a mother, when my son was just a few months old, I entered a different kind of painful waiting in discernment and decision-making. As a new mom I really didn't want to take on new risks or challenges, yet I felt God edging me away from my comfort zone. But I was stuck. I felt afraid of making a wrong investment with the opportunities I had been given, wondering if I could really do what I thought was being asked of me.

Then one morning in prayer I remembered that sermon and sensed Jesus's invitation to fix my eyes on him. I could see myself as that toddler learning to walk. I had been obsessively looking at the ground, fearful and fretting, unable to move. But when I looked up, I was captured by the *joy* on Jesus's face, and I suddenly felt the energy and urgency to walk forward. While I couldn't see into the future, I was assured that the One who could saw something good and beautiful there, and was beckoning me to come join him in it. Now, nearly a decade later, I am in another season of waiting and discernment (they keep coming, don't they?), and while the fears and opportunities are different, the invitation is the same.

I've come to call this experience *borrowing joy from the future*, and it has opened me up to a truth I should have realized all along. This is always what God has made available to us! We have been invited into *God's* story, into *God's* future. When we declare that Jesus is Lord, we are confessing that in this story God gets to write the ending—and it is *good*.

So there is a joyful certainty out ahead, whether it is in my lifetime or not. And the joyful certainty is that God's good kingdom will indeed come! One day, everything we are now waiting for will be reality. There will be no more death, sickness, tears, or oppression. There will be no violence or isolation, and all will be *well*. God's good and beautiful dream for God's creation will be fully realized, and every tribe and tongue will be united in worship. God's kingdom *will* come, and his will *will* be done on earth as it is in heaven!

This is the joyful future that awaits us, no matter what our present looks like. But in God's grace, God doesn't leave that joy only in the future. As we fix our eyes on Jesus, we experience the miraculous truth that God's joy is rushing from the future into our present. God shares joy with us so we can participate in God's joyful future *now*. We may borrow joy from the future, but God is the one who lends it to us—and God doesn't ask for it back!

QUESTIONS FOR REFLECTION, DISCUSSION, AND PRAYER

What comes to your mind when you think of fixing your eyes on Jesus?

....

....

....

....

....

....

....

....

....

....

....

....

....

....

....

Where and how do you need God to lend you God's joy right now?

....

....

....

....

....

....

....

....

....

....

....

What good gifts fill you with gratitude today?

....

....

....

....

....

....

....

....

....

....

....

Rest & Reflect

Look back at the writings from this week. Which scripture, idea, or story stands out to you as most meaningful or most challenging? Take time to revisit it and listen for the Spirit's invitation to go deeper.

What have you learned about yourself and/or about God as you've practiced gratitude this week?

....

....

....

....

....

....

....

....

....

....

....

....

....

How have you recognized the fruit of joy growing within you this week?

....

....

....

....

....

....

....

....

....

....

What practices or ideas from this week do you want to take with you as regular practices for your life?

....

....

....

....

....

....

....

....

....

....

DECEMBER 22, 2024

My soul glorifies the Lord
and my spirit rejoices in God my Savior,
for he has been mindful
of the humble state of his servant.

He has brought down rulers from their thrones
but has lifted up the humble.
He has filled the hungry with good things
but has sent the rich away empty.

—LUKE 1:46B–48A, 52–53

We've arrived in the final week of Advent, where we are invited to explore the gift of peace. Seasons of waiting can often be tense with uncertainty, even downright tumultuous. Like joy, we expect the tranquility of peace to come only after what we're waiting for has arrived. But in Advent, we are invited to reconsider our expectations of peace—not just how it arrives but also what it *is*. I expect peace to bring the comfortable tranquility of a conflict-free zone. But when I encounter the words in Mary's "Magnificat," I confess it sounds more disruptive than calming to me. Hearing the bold conviction of this young woman's words is my first indication that God's definition of peace is far greater than my own.

In her prophetic song, Mary echoes the prophets who spoke of righteousness (*sedaqah*), justice (*mishpat*), and peace (*shalom*) as truths that are inseparably woven together. Righteousness enacts God's desire for justice, which brings holistic peace and well-being for both individuals and communities. The Hebrew word *shalom* is understood as the presence of wholeness and rightness, all things being as God intends them to be. God's promise of peace is far greater than the absence of conflict—it is putting things right.

For prophets like Amos, Micah, and Isaiah, this vision of *shalom* had both social and economic implications. They consistently called God's people toward loving compassion by sharing their wealth and privilege with the poorest and most vulnerable among them, rebuking those in power who only acted to benefit themselves. But they also promised that when God's people were committed to righteousness and enacted justice, collective *shalom* would be the natural result.

Like the prophets before her, Mary's words point to *shalom* within the injustices of her society. In Roman-occupied Palestine, justice was definitely *not* rolling like a river nor righteousness like a never-ending stream (see Amos 5:24). Those who sat on thrones of political and religious power used their privilege to get away with injustice and oppression. Mary knew that God's Messiah growing in her womb would live out a righteousness that carried the twin gifts of *justice* and *peace* into this troubled reality.

Thirty some years later, Jesus preached a message of justice and peace that surprised even those who thought they knew what those words meant. He talked of loving one's enemy, a commitment to nonviolence, and being a person of integrity no matter the cost (Matthew 5:33–48). So when Jesus said "blessed are the peacemakers," he wasn't encouraging people to play nice and never ruffle any feathers. He taught that true peace is made by doing the work of justice in partnership with God to bring things into the way they should be. Those who do this, Jesus said, are known as God's children (Matthew 5:9) because they've joined the family business that was established in the garden.

What does this expanded definition of peace mean for those of us who wait? In my own waiting, I notice an internal tug-of-war between two reactionary stances. The first is a fiery zeal to make peace all by myself by taking justice into my own hands; the second is despair-induced inaction, believing I am powerless against the injustices that hinder *shalom*. In the first response I am tempted to wait for no one; in the second response I am tempted to sit on my hands while I wait for God to do it all in some far-off future.

Thankfully, Jesus names a third way, inviting us into humble, patient participation with the Prince of Peace. This happens as we open ourselves to God's *shalom* flourishing in us and as God teaches us God's ways of justice that extend *shalom* to others. In this final week of Advent, may we be open to the full breadth of the Spirit's peace-making work in us.

QUESTIONS FOR REFLECTION, DISCUSSION, AND PRAYER

How does the concept of *shalom* as described here challenge or confirm your understanding of peace?

....

....

....

....

....

....

....

....

....

....

....

....

....

....

....

....

....

....

Where have you seen a commitment to justice bring peace to individuals and communities?

....
....
....
....
....
....
....
....
....
....
....
....
....
....
....
....
....
....
....
....
....
....

What places in your own life, relationships, or community are in need of God's *shalom* right now?

....

....

....

....

....

....

....

....

....

....

....

....

....

....

....

....

....

....

....

....

....

....

....

Nothing Will Hurt or Destroy

SCRIPTURE

ISAIAH 11

In that day the wolf and the lamb will live together;
the leopard will lie down with the baby goat.
The calf and the yearling will be safe with the lion,
and a little child will lead them all.
The cow will graze near the bear.
The cub and the calf will lie down together.
The lion will eat hay like a cow.
The baby will play safely near the hole of a cobra.
Yes, a little child will put its hand in a nest
of deadly snakes without harm.
Nothing will hurt or destroy in all my holy mountain,
for as the waters fill the sea,
*so the earth will be filled with people who know the L*ORD.

—ISAIAH 11:6–9 (NLT)

When it comes to embracing God's *shalom* vision of peace on earth, our greatest obstacle might just be our inability to imagine it. Maybe that's why Isaiah wrote about it in poetry, a language better suited to stirring imagination than giving instructions.

The prophet-poet paints a picture that is both shocking and beautiful of safety and belonging for all amidst a vast array of differences and would-be enemies. I tend to assume that peace comes as a result of sameness, which seems to be a common human assumption. This is probably why we tend to gather in likeminded groups and create boundaries to keep ourselves separate from those who are different. But God's vision of peaceful community is not one of uniformity and segmentation.

Instead, Isaiah describes a place where all creatures have full access to all parts of God's holy mountain. No one gets to claim territory or parcel out pieces of land for themselves. Instead, belonging is extended equally to all who are present. Isaiah's vision shows us what it looks like when, to borrow Paul's words written centuries later, the walls of hostility that once maintained divisions have been torn down (see Ephesians 2:14). Without hostility or division, there is a complete lack of violence—everyone on God's mountain even seems to enjoy one another! Each creature values and protects the others, from the strongest to the most vulnerable.

This picture seems so far from the realm of possibility that I don't have the capacity to imagine it on my own. But as I spend time with these words, my imagination expands, and I begin to recognize and long for the kind of peace God has in mind. Situations that may once have felt chaotic or unfamiliar instead become the very places where I see God's kingdom showing up on earth as it is in heaven.

My years in recovery ministry taught me a little about this kind of peace. Women and men from every conceivable walk of life gathered weekly in a shared commitment of honesty, safety, and trust. No one was the same, but all were united in a shared need of God and readiness for transformation. The peace experienced in that space was an active, often messy peace that birthed numerous stories of wholeness, healing, belonging, and restoration in our community. God's kingdom of peace is made real on earth wherever the church of Jesus Christ gathers in our full, glorious diversity as our differences are equally valued and celebrated.

Isaiah's poem ends by giving the closest thing to instructions a poet can provide: God's vision of peace is made possible because all people know God. Somehow, when we fully know the God of peace—the God who creates safety and belonging for all—we will be at peace with one another too.

May our imaginations expand to dream God's dream, and may God's dream be realized in us.

QUESTIONS FOR REFLECTION, DISCUSSION, AND PRAYER

How does Isaiah's vision challenge or confirm your own imagination for peace?

....

....

....

....

....

....

....

....

....

....

Where have you seen God's vision of peace in a community of belonging and safety amidst great diversity?

....
....
....
....
....
....
....
....
....
....
....

What barriers keep you from being at peace with those who are different from you?

....
....
....
....
....
....
....
....
....
....

Where You Go I Will Go

SCRIPTURE

RUTH 1

But Ruth replied, "Don't urge me to leave you or to turn back from you. Where you go I will go, and where you stay I will stay. Your people will be my people and your God my God. Where you die I will die, and there I will be buried. May the Lᴏʀᴅ deal with me, be it ever so severely, if even death separates you and me." When Naomi realized that Ruth was determined to go with her, she stopped urging her.

—RUTH 1:16–18

Ruth's whole story happens in a season of immense grief, transition, and uncertainty. It tells us about Naomi, a woman who experienced an extreme lack of *shalom* in her life: first in famine, then as a refugee, and finally as the lone survivor of her husband and adult sons. Furthermore, we are told that this story happens during the period of the judges, which is akin to painting the darkest background imaginable. Those were days of lawless chaos and violence for the people of Israel—an image as opposite to *shalom* as there could possibly be.

But somehow Ruth seems impervious to the despair that surrounds her. She is adamant about accompanying Naomi back to her homeland, a journey that will take Ruth away from hers. Ruth could end her own period of suffering and waiting, and move on with her life. But she chooses to unite her story to Naomi's, joining in all Naomi's troubles. She offers Naomi something like a marriage vow, giving us the strongest words of covenantal love uttered by a human in all of the Old Testament.

In the months that follow, Ruth lives out this commitment and then some. In her, we see a love that rolls up its sleeves and gets to work, literally doing manual labor to put food on their table. Ruth's constant care for Naomi restores well-being little by little. Her work ethic also catches the attention of Boaz, the wealthy landowner who makes way for Ruth to harvest grain from his fields. While others may have run her off their property as a thieving immigrant, Boaz recognizes her as a woman of virtue who has dedicated her life to caring for Naomi.

The rest of the story unfolds as a chain reaction of *chesed,* each act laying another brick in the sturdy shelter of *shalom.* Boaz sees and celebrates what Ruth is doing and decides to bless her. He gives more than he is required, just as Ruth gave to Naomi. Ruth then recognizes Boaz as a co-conspirator in *chesed* and learns to trust him. Eventually she trusts him enough to offer a supremely risky marriage proposal, which Boaz agrees to. This was the ultimate way Ruth could provide a future not only for herself but also for Naomi, whose family line could continue through her. By the end of this short story, the heaviness of waiting is replaced by the joyful anticipation of a new child.

In Scripture, *chesed* is most often used to talk about the love God offers to us. But here we get a picture of what happens when humans are empowered to love like God loves. When we practice self-giving love with a willingness to take risks on behalf of the other, well-being and wholeness are restored in individuals and the community. The woman in deepest grief and despair is not left alone to fend for herself. The least likely person (the foreigner) defies all prejudices and is found to be the most virtuous and heroic of all. A man with privilege acts with generosity and uses his position to care for those who have none. A community learns to trust an outsider, extending belonging to the immigrant. All of this *chesed* made way for Jesus to be born from this lineage generations later in the very same town of Bethlehem, where angels declare the good news of *peace on earth*.

Chesed love brings about *shalom* peace. May it be so in us.

QUESTIONS FOR REFLECTION, DISCUSSION, AND PRAYER

With which character in this story do you identify most—Naomi, Ruth, or Boaz? Why?

....

....

....

....

....

....

....

....

....

....

....

....

....

....

....

When have you seen a commitment to love (*chesed*) that restored well-being (*shalom*)?

....

....

....

....

....

....

....

....

....

....

How are you being invited to receive or bring peace through the work of love today?

....

....

....

....

....

....

....

....

....

....

....

Son of David, Have Mercy

SCRIPTURE

LUKE 18:35–43; LUKE 19:1–10

*As Jesus approached Jericho, a blind man was sitting
by the roadside begging. When he heard the crowd going by,
he asked what was happening. They told him,
"Jesus of Nazareth is passing by."*

He called out, "Jesus, Son of David, have mercy on me!"

*Those who led the way rebuked him and told him to be quiet,
but he shouted all the more, "Son of David, have mercy on me!"*

Jesus stopped and ordered the man to be brought to him.

—*LUKE 18:35–40*

*When Jesus reached the spot, he looked up and said to him,
"Zacchaeus, come down immediately. I must stay at your house
today." So he came down at once and welcomed him gladly.
All the people saw this and began to mutter,
"He has gone to be the guest of a sinner."*

—*LUKE 19:5–7*

On the surface it would appear that Zacchaeus and the blind beggar have nothing in common, yet both are marginalized in their hometown of Jericho. Zacchaeus is hated because he is an accomplice to the Roman occupation, gathering heavy taxes from his neighbors to send to Rome while paying himself handsomely in the process. The blind man may not be hated, but he too asks his neighbors for money, and is easily dismissed. One is wealthy and able-bodied, the other disabled and impoverished. But they hold this in common: neither is at peace.

All of Jesus's ministry can be seen as a restoration of *shalom*—making things right and whole, the way they should be. But this work of making peace takes many different forms because there are many different forces that disrupt it. And the events of that day in Jericho show us that sometimes making peace is itself rather disruptive.

The disruption in this story begins with the blind man calling out from the side of the road. I can imagine a large, happy crowd all around Jesus, hanging on every word, proud as can be that he is coming to their city. But it seems they are not keen on introducing Jesus to their town beggar. Maybe they are embarrassed or think his cries are inappropriate. Maybe they want to protect Jesus from inconvenience, or think this blind beggar makes Jericho look bad.

Whatever their reasons, the crowd tries to silence him. But the man persists, and Jesus stops to listen. Then he invites the man to join him, disrupting the processional. The disruptive cry from the margins is brought to center stage, where Jesus engages the man in conversation as an equal and heals his blindness.

Then, just a few steps down the road, another disruption occurs. This time it's caused by Jesus calling out to a man who would otherwise remain hidden on the sidelines. Even still, Zacchaeus is a willing and gracious host, while his neighbors are fit to be tied. Their sense of propriety is also disrupted because how could Jesus spend time with such a terrible person as Zacchaeus?! The final act of disruption comes from Zacchaeus himself as he has a change of heart and disrupts his own accumulation of wealth. His commitment to restitution is an act of justice that makes peace throughout the city.

If we only recognize peace as tranquility and orderliness, we will never see the work of peacemaking in disruptive stories of tension and conflict. But if we understand that *shalom* comes in making things right in people and communities, we begin to see that disruption is actually part of the journey to peace! By disrupting what is normal, Jesus brings both men to a place of holistic well-being. As a result, the whole community is set on a trajectory of shared belonging and restoration.

Like the people of Jericho, we often prioritize tranquility and call it peace. Jesus, on the other hand, will not be satisfied with anything less than peace that offers the fullness of well-being—for us and for our neighbors.

QUESTIONS FOR REFLECTION, DISCUSSION, AND PRAYER

How do you respond to the idea that disruption is sometimes necessary for making peace?

....

....

....

....

....

....

....

....

....

....

Consider how you are similar to Zacchaeus, the blind man, and/or the crowd in Jericho. How is Jesus extending peace and well-being where you are?

....
....
....
....
....
....
....
....
....
....

Where are you experiencing disruption now? What kind of peace might lie at the end?

....
....
....
....
....
....
....
....
....
....

The Peace of God

SCRIPTURE

JOHN 14:15–31; PHILIPPIANS 4

*But the Advocate, the Holy Spirit, whom the Father will send
in my name, will teach you all things and will remind you of
everything I have said to you. Peace I leave with you;
my peace I give you. I do not give to you as the world gives.
Do not let your hearts be troubled and do not be afraid.*

—JOHN 14:26–27

*Do not be anxious about anything, but in every situation,
by prayer and petition, with thanksgiving,
present your requests to God. And the peace of God,
which transcends all understanding,
will guard your hearts and your minds in Christ Jesus.*

—PHILIPPIANS 4:6–7

Recently I heard from a friend who called to tell me she's going on an end-of-life plan under hospice care. She's only in her forties but has battled chronic illness for more than ten years, and her doctors finally admitted they were out of new things to try. After such a long time fighting illness, I asked her how she and her husband had come to this difficult decision. She paused for a long moment, then said, "Well, you know that peace that passes understanding? We have that." I marvel at my beautiful friend who is willing to walk forward into death, knowing the peace that is with her now will be with her forever.

The peace that transcends all understanding is a really good name for it. How could we possibly understand the kind of peace that persists when there are seemingly no signs of peace on the horizon? It's the kind of peace that completely befuddles the oppressors of martyrs and the persecuted church. It's the kind of peace that, as gospel singer-songwriter Shirley Caesar and so many choirs have sung about, "the world didn't give to me, and the world can't take it away." Christ's peace is surely the gift unlike anything else the world gives. It's peace no one can take away because the gift is a person who decides to stay. Our Advocate, Comforter, Holy Spirit, third Person of the triune God is *with us* always, no matter what. This is the source of our peace.

God's intention for all God's creation is *shalom*—wholeness and well-being, safety and belonging for all. While we long for it to be apparent in all relationships and places on earth, *shalom* is not dependent on external factors. Our deepest sense of well-being comes from *within* us, radiating from that very place in which Christ has made his home. With the peace of Christ ruling our hearts (Colossians 3:15) and guarding our minds, we can be people who are settled, assured of our belonging, and held in the eternal safety of God's love. This gift of peace empowers us, like the Jesus we follow, to walk even through the worst of injustice and death without surrendering our deepest well-being. We can be in pain, we can certainly lament, and we can even be angry and confused. But we will never be abandoned.

Writing during the intense political turmoil and international plague of the twelfth century, Julian of Norwich was given her own vision of God's peace. She wrote, "I saw that God is our true peace; and he is our safe protector when we ourselves are in disquiet, and he constantly works to bring us into endless peace."[1] We are always being invited into the ongoing project of God's peace, in our lives and in our world. Even in the midst of waiting for the chaos of war and division to end, the

---

1. Julian of Norwich, *The Showings*, trans. Edmund College and James Walsh (Mahwah, NJ: Paulist Press, 1978), 265.

peace of Christ is with us. And in us, the people of peace, the watching world sees a gift that may prompt the question: where did you get that?

QUESTIONS FOR REFLECTION, DISCUSSION, AND PRAYER

When have you experienced the peace that passes all understanding—or witnessed it in someone else?

....

....

....

....

....

....

....

....

....

....

....

....

....

....

....

....

....

How does it provide you peace to imagine God being fully present with you now?

....

....

....

....

....

....

....

....

....

....

....

How or when have you been a person of peace? How can you be a person of peace going forward?

....

....

....

....

....

....

....

....

....

....

....

....

FRIDAY

Rest & Reflect

Look back at the readings from this week. Which scripture, idea, or story stands out to you as most meaningful or most challenging? Take time to revisit it and listen for the Spirit's invitation to go deeper.

What have you learned about yourself and/or God this week?

....

....

....

....

....

....

....

....

....

....

....

....

....

How have you recognized the presence of peace in your life this week? Where have you encountered your need for peace?

....
....
....
....
....
....
....
....
....
....

What practices or ideas from this week do you want to take with you as regular practices for your life?

....
....
....
....
....
....
....
....
....
....

Are We There Yet?

Merry Christmas! The longing of Advent ends with the celebration of Jesus's birth on December 25. Now we transition into a season of celebration during the twelve days of Christmas and beyond. These are days of joy and light, time spent cherishing the good gifts we've been waiting for. But our own seasons of waiting do not magically end every December 25—if only they would! The calendar moves ahead, but our lives rarely keep exact time with the seasons marching on. Those of us who began Advent in a season of waiting will most likely continue to be in a season of waiting as it ends.

But just as Advent is not a countdown to Christmas, neither are our lives just a countdown to getting what we want. In our waiting we grow, we find good gifts, and we become more like the King for whom we watch and wait. In many ways this four-week-long journey of Advent is our annual refresher on how we live the rest of the year. Advent teaches us *how* to wait, reminds us what we are waiting for, and gives us new eyes to recognize the ways God comes even before the wait is over. No, we aren't there yet. Our journey continues. But we are getting closer! We who live the way of Jesus are journeying into ongoing transformation as we become more and more like the One we follow.

This thing Jesus has invited us into is literally a *way of life* that includes a lot of waiting. That is not to say we will continue to experience more of the same. It's not the same because *we* are not the same! We have been, and will continue to be, changed as we wait. This Advent, the Spirit has been at work growing the fruit of hope, love, joy, and peace in you. These gifts aren't like the things we open and stick on a shelf or use up until they're gone. They are signs of the Spirit's ongoing work within us—the work that our God will surely be faithful to complete (see Philippians 1:6).

As you walk forward into whatever is next, consider what has been growing within you over the last four weeks. How is the Spirit inviting you to tend to this new growth? Perhaps you will be led to join in solidarity with the lament of others to strengthen hope in places of despair. Or maybe you will be invited to take on a regular practice of gratitude that cultivates joy, or experience new ways of letting yourself be loved. The Spirit may also lead you to specific acts of justice so that *shalom* can flourish in you and your community.

Whatever we do, it is in concert with what the Spirit does first. We are not in control of our own transformation, but it certainly cannot happen without us either. As we move forward into the promises and unknowns of the future, receive these words of benediction from nineteenth-century Jesuit priest and theologian Pierre Teilhard de Chardin:

Above all, trust in the slow work of God.
We are quite naturally impatient in everything to reach the end
  without delay.
We should like to skip the intermediate stages.
We are impatient of being on the way to something unknown,
  something new.
And yet it is the law of all progress
  that it is made by passing through
  some stages of instability—
  and that it may take a very long time.
And so I think it is with you;
  your ideas mature gradually—let them grow,
  let them shape themselves, without undue haste.
Don't try to force them on,
  as though you could be today what time
  (that is to say, grace and circumstances acting on your own
    good will)
  will make of you tomorrow.
Only God could say what this new spirit
  gradually forming within you will be.
Give our Lord the benefit of believing
  that his hand is leading you,
  and accept the anxiety of feeling yourself
  in suspense and incomplete.[1]

1. Pierre Teilhard de Chardin, SJ, "Patient Trust," *Hearts on Fire: Praying with Jesuits*, ed.
Michael Harter, SJ (Chicago: Loyola Press, 1993), 58.

QUESTIONS FOR REFLECTION, DISCUSSION, AND PRAYER

How would you describe what you are taking with you as you depart the season of Advent? Write a few short sentences to summarize this journey that will serve as a reminder and witness to your future self.

....

....

....

....

....

....

....

....

....

....

....

....

....

....

....

....

....

....

....

....

Which one virtue—hope, love, joy, or peace—seems most important for your journey ahead? How will you partner with the Spirit to nurture this good fruit growing in you?

....

....

....

....

....

....

....

....

....

How do you respond to the exhortation to trust in God's slow work? Where do you struggle to believe God's hand is leading you?

....

....

....

....

....

....

....

....

....

....

As you look ahead, what do you feel you need? Write or speak your prayer to God as you transition into the holidays, and the season beyond.

....
....
....
....
....
....
....
....
....
....
....
....
....
....
....
....
....
....
....
....
....
....
....
....

Acknowledgments

Although I did not write during Advent, this project accompanied me during a trying season of my own waiting. I am grateful for the many ways the Spirit produced good fruit in me while I wrote. I am also aware of the many people who walked with me into hope, love, joy, and peace during these months.

My husband, Brent, is my greatest friend and encourager and has offered me countless words of wisdom to make this little book the best it could be.

I am indebted to my friends Janie and Ursula for reading all my first drafts and giving generous and thoughtful feedback, and to the many friends who allowed me to use portions of our conversations in these pages.

There are also those I cannot name who committed to praying for me in this work, and I know the Spirit has been at work through you. Thank you to these friends and the many others who have walked this journey with me.

And thanks be to God, whose gifts are so good and so numerous that the work of writing on them will never be done!